SECRETS
OF
WINTER

Carron Brown

Illustrated by Georgina Tee

Kane Miller
A DIVISION OF EDC PUBLISHING

A winter's night is bustling with life.

If you look closely through the dark trees, around the icy river, and in the snowy hollows, you will find lots of activity.

Shine a flashlight behind the page, or hold it up to the light to reveal what is hidden in a wintery nighttime woodland. Discover a world of great surprises.

In the fall, many trees lose their leaves.
Can you see who is sleeping here?

Bzzzzzz . . . Shhhhhh.

This bumblebee scooped out a hole in the earth. She will sleep until spring.

Snow is falling.
Look closely
at the flakes.

Can you see
their shapes?

Every snowflake
has six sides.

But each
flake has a
different pattern.

Whoosh!

What has landed
in the tree?

A flock of waxwings.
They eat the tree's berries.

This waxwing has found a berry on the ground.

Who is sleeping under the rock?

A wood frog is asleep.
The icy weather might
freeze the frog, but it
will thaw out again.

Snow covers the land.

What has made these tracks?

Brrrrr!

A hare snuggles up to keep warm.

Her white fur hides her in the snow. In the summer, her fur is brown.

A red squirrel peeps
inside the tree.

What is he looking for?

Crunch!

There's a store of nuts in a hollow.
The nuts were hidden here in the fall.

These catkins are the seeds
of a birch tree. Who is eating them?

A grouse.

She has extra
feathers on
her feet.

They are like
snowshoes.

Ivy covers this tree.
There are creatures
asleep here.
Can you see them?

Tiny snails curl
up inside their
shells all winter.

They seal
themselves in

so they don't
dry out.

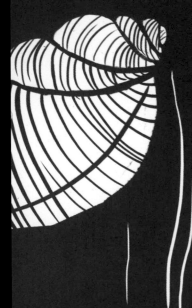

A fox is asleep
on the snow.

Can you see her face?

The fox's big, bushy tail keeps her face and paws warm.

The lake is frozen,
but something is
moving under the ice.

Can you see anything?

Most fish lie near the
bottom of the lake.
The water is warmer here.

Evergreen trees have leaves all year long.
Who is sheltering from the snow?

A family of deer is eating the new leaves on the trees.

Munch!

Red berries shine bright against the snow.
Who will eat this fruit?

Berries make a tasty meal for a mouse.

He can climb to reach fruit higher up.

The mouse is
running to hide.

Can you see why?

Swoop!

The mouse has spotted a
hungry owl just in time.

The owl eats small animals!

Another creature is
hiding from the owl.
Can you see it?

It's a weasel standing
in the hollow stump of
an old tree.

He is very good
at hiding.

There's a large hole under this old tree.
Take a look inside...

Bears sleep all winter.

They will wake up in the
Spring when there are
lots of insects to eat.

Zzzz . . .

Zzzzzzz!

As the sun rises,
the nighttime animals
go to sleep while the
daytime creatures wake up.

The animals that sleep
through the winter will
doze until spring.

There's more...

Animals and plants have different ways of staying alive in the cold winter. Look carefully in the fall and you can spot them getting ready.

Changing color The fur and feathers of some animals turn white and grow thicker, too. This helps them hide in the snow and stay warm. The white hare turns from brown to white in the winter.

Leaf fall Trees prepare for the winter, too. Many lose their leaves in the fall. The tough bark is watertight and can survive the winter cold. Delicate fruit and leaf buds won't grow until the warmer spring.

Long sleep Bears and other animals hibernate—they sleep all winter. They eat and eat in the fall to build up fat to keep them alive. Their heartbeat slows down while they sleep so they use less energy.

Awake at night Animals that are awake at night and sleep during the day are called nocturnal. Foxes, for example, hunt for food in the early morning and evening. They sleep curled up in the winter to keep warm.

Food stores Animals that eat seeds and plants gather as much as they can in the fall, storing it in underground burrows or in tree hollows. Squirrels store food in their cheeks until they can hide or bury it.

Shelter Many animals need to shelter during the cold winter weather. Deer shelter beneath leafy trees, under hedges and in long grass to keep safe and warm.

Snowshoes Some animals have feet that don't sink into the snow. Snowshoe hares have toes that spread wide to help them walk on top of it. Some birds, like the grouse, have extra feathers on their feet to help them do the same.

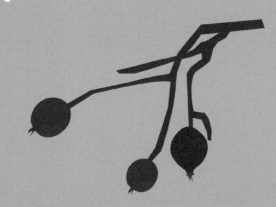

Waiting for spring Most flowers and other plants don't grow in the winter, but animals can still find food to eat. Berries are a type of fruit that grow in the winter. Bulbs and seeds, however, wait until it is warmer.

First American Edition 2015
Kane Miller, A Division of EDC Publishing

Copyright © 2017 Quarto Publishing plc

For information contact:
Kane Miller, A Division of EDC Publishing
5402 S 122nd E Ave
Tulsa, OK 74146
www.kanemiller.com
www.myubam.com

Library of Congress Control Number: 2014950264

Printed in China

ISBN: 978-1-61067-369-3

8 9 10